MOOSE

Moose Magic for Kids

For all my Sister's children.
              – Jeff Fair

**For a free color catalog describing Gareth Stevens' list of high-quality books, call
1-800-542-2595 (USA) or 1-800-461-9120 (Canada). Gareth Stevens' Fax: 414-225-0377.**

Library of Congress Cataloging-in-Publication Data

Fair, Jeff.
    Moose magic for kids / by Jeff Fair ; photography by Michael H. Francis ; illustrated by Sandy Stevens.
        p. cm. — (Animal magic for kids)
    Based on: Moose for kids. 1992.
    Includes index.
    Summary: Describes the habitat, physical characteristics, and behavior of the moose of the wild north
country.
    ISBN-0-8368-1376-6
    1. Moose—Juvenile literature. [1. Moose.] I. Francis, Michael H. (Michael Harlowe), 1953- ill.
II. Stevens, Sandy, ill. III. Fair, Jeff. Moose for kids. IV. Title. V. Title: Moose. VI. Series.
QL737.U55F353   1995
599.73'57—dc20   95-16311

This edition first published in 1995 by
Gareth Stevens Publishing
1555 North RiverCenter Drive, Suite 201
Milwaukee, Wisconsin 53212 USA

Based on the book, *Moose for Kids*, text © 1992 by Jeff Fair, all photographs © 1992 by
Michael H. Francis except pp. 6, 10, 28, 44, © Robert W. Baldwin, with illustrations by
Sandy Stevens.   First published in the United States in 1992 by NorthWord Press, Inc.,
Minocqua, Wisconsin. End matter © 1995 by Gareth Stevens, Inc.

Printed in the United States of America

1 2 3 4 5 6 7 8 9 99 98 97 96 95

by Jeff Fair

MOOSE

Moose Magic for Kids

Gareth Stevens Publishing
MILWAUKEE

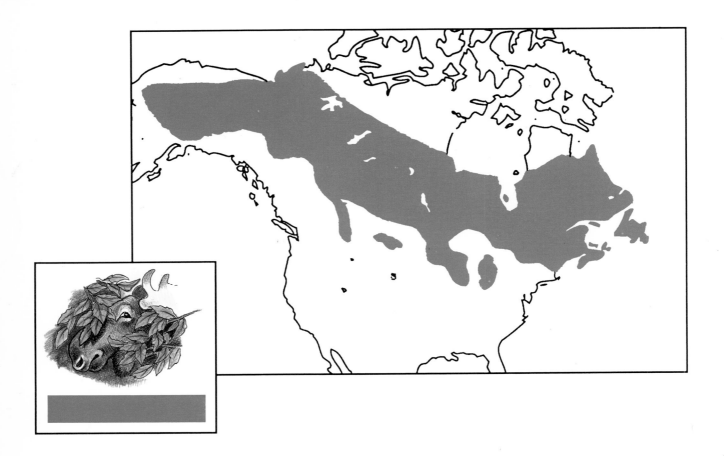

The great northwoods stretches from Maine and Labrador to Alaska.
Smell the evergreen air and the moldy aroma of muck from the marsh.
Around us, deep forests of spruce and fir hold silence and secrets.
You could get lost for a long time in this country, if you wanted to.
Wild things live here: loons and ravens and wolves. Bears belong to
these woods, and mink frogs live in the bogs. But moose symbolize
the wild north country best of all. This country is their home.

Moose make their meals from plants that grow here. They need the cool woods and open waters to survive summer's heat. This north-country landscape contains marshes and muskeg bogs, lakes and ponds, and meadows in the vast forest made when lightning has kindled a fire or loggers have cut down trees. The best moose foods grow in these meadows.

The native Algonquians, Indian people of the north country, gave the moose its name many years ago. Moose means "he who eats off trees and shrubs," or simply "twig eater." Algonquians believed that moose were good omens. If you dream of moose often, they said, you will live long.

The moose supplied the Algonquian people with many of the things they needed. Its hide became their clothing and shelter. From its bones and antlers, they fashioned tools. Its flesh—up to 700 pounds of muscle from a single moose—fed a native family all through the long northern winter.

You might say we still consider moose to be good omens, although most people today just say they feel lucky to see one. Moose provide some of us with food and mittens, and they give all of us something to marvel at. Mounted moose heads (with those glass eyes that follow you around) hang in places of honor in many north-country lodges. We wonder how such a large creature keeps itself secret and makes its living in the harsh wilderness of the northwoods.

7

You'd recognize a moose, wouldn't you? Watch for an animal as big as a horse, with four long, skinny legs. If it has a long head with a little beard (called a dewlap) at its throat, big ears like a mule, a drooping nose in front and a tiny tail hidden in back, then you've found a moose. And if you see a set of antlers attached in front of its ears, then it's a male, called a bull moose. A big rack of antlers is the crown of this king of the northwoods.

The awesome size of a moose makes your knees wobble when you see one. A big moose stands six feet tall at its shoulders and weighs more than 1,000 pounds. That's heavier than four refrigerators.

But you have to look hard to find one. Moose are brown, usually dark brown, the same color as marsh mud and forest shadows. And despite their huge size, moose move through the woods as quietly as shadows. Moose prefer to travel alone and stick to the wilder country. They usually appear when you don't expect them to. Moose are like that.

To really look for a moose, keep a sharp eye out for antlers, ripples on the pond, and big old tree stumps that walk. Watch for the signs it leaves behind. Moose make a lot of footprints in snow and soft ground. These hoof tracks help us find moose, or at least know where they've been. A moose track looks like a heart, or like a pair of teardrops about six inches long. The sharper end of each track points in the direction that the moose traveled.

In winter, moose leave behind piles of round or oval pellets bigger than large grapes. These pellets are really just packed sawdust, and they don't smell like anything you couldn't bring home.

In the summer, moose droppings may be softer because moose eat softer, fresher plants at this time of year. They look like what you might find behind a happy Hereford cow. Call them moose pies. On a sunny hillside, you may notice a faint barnyard perfume. But there are no cattle in these woods. It's moose sign that you smell. Follow your nose. And watch where you step—you might learn something.

Now look over here. See the big patch of grass matted down in the meadow? Why, it's the size of your mattress at home. But this is a moose bed instead. If we had been quieter, we might have caught the moose snoozing.

11

In the muddy north-country spring, when cackling geese return on the warm wind and loons come back to dance, moose leave the drier forests and slip into the moist muskegs and thickets of young aspen. After the long, hungry winter, moose begin to fatten up again on a diet of fresh new leaves and stems of willow, aspen, and maple.

Moose won't reach very far for their food. They browse on leaves and twigs between four and ten feet above the ground—easy pickings for the long-legged moose. You won't catch a moose grazing on grass very often. Grass is a long way down from a moose mouth. With such long front legs and such a short neck, a moose has to kneel to touch the ground with its muzzle.

A moose has front teeth on the bottom, but not on top. It partly cuts and partly tears off each bite of browse. To reach higher twigs, a moose sometimes walks right up to a small tree, straddles it between his front legs, and keeps walking, bending the tree over. When he reaches the top of the tree, he eats his fill. When he walks away, the tree springs back up. It looks as though the moose had to be twelve feet tall to reach up there. This is as close as a moose will come to playing a trick on you.

13

Moose eat the smooth bark of aspen and maple trees, too. They scrape the bark right off the tree and into their mouths with the two front teeth on their lower jaw. Afterward, the tree looks as though someone scraped its trunk with two sharp spoons, side by side. You may be close to a moose if you find white, moist wood beneath these scraped places. Check for tracks. Stand very still. Is a moose watching you? Maybe. Moose are like that.

You may not find the moose, but you can be pretty sure that it will return next year in the same season. Moose rove around for different foods at different times of year, but they don't go more than a few miles away. If no one puts up a shopping center or plunks down a highway where you find your moose sign, the moose will probably be back next year.

In May and June you won't see many cow moose. Most of them are pregnant now. Pregnant cows find secret places near lakeshores and on small islands. Here they give birth to their calves, usually single ones, but sometimes twins. The reddish-brown moose calves weigh only 25 to 35 pounds, and they arrive with four long, wobbly legs that are hard to control at first. A cow licks its calf a lot, and the two stick close together. By its third or fourth day, a moose calf could outrun you, but before that it would make an easy meal for a bear or a pack of wolves if its mother weren't there to protect it.

A defensive cow moose lays back her ears, lowers her head, and runs
between her calf and whatever threatens it. Long hairs on the back of
her neck and shoulders stand up like a dark mane. The threat might
be a bear poking around in the pasture. Or it might be a pack of wolves
challenging her from several sides. Or the threat might even be you, if
you surprise the cow moose. The cow can kick high and hard up front
and like a mule in back. An angry moose is a tough critter to argue
with. Many bears and wolves decide to go elsewhere and look for an
easier meal.

Moose look pretty scruffy in late spring. Big patches of last year's hair peel off to make way for a dark new coat. You might find a patch of moose hair hanging in alder branches or floating at the water's edge. The long, hollow guard hairs feel like the bristles of a brush and twist like rope between your fingers. By next winter, the new guard hairs will be up to eight or ten inches long. Between them, underneath, the moose will grow a warm, wooly undercoat.

Calves follow the cows out of hiding as soon as they have their legs under control. By tagging along closely, they learn to swim and to chew on the right plants. Moose calves don't stay little for long. First they grow taller, then they grow longer. Their bones will grow for seven years, but they grow fastest during that first summer. By autumn, when they stop nursing, moose calves weigh 400 pounds.

Wildlife of another kind thrives in the northwoods during the warm season. On quiet evenings you hear them by the millions, revving their little engines. Black flies, deer flies, moose flies, and mosquitoes torment anything with blood. You'll want to bring plenty of bug repellent, even though it never really works, and maybe some mosquito netting to cover your head. Moose bat at bugs with their big ears or go swimming to be left in peace. Mostly, moose just put up with bugs. Moose are like that.

Summer is a good time to see a moose or two in the water. A cow and her calf, maybe. Or a couple of young bulls who have learned to put up with each other. They cool off in the water and eat the juicy pond weeds.

Look for moose in the early morning and at dusk, especially after storms and when the wind dies down. On a quiet day you might hear one over in the bay, mucking around on those saucer-sized hooves and bobbing for lilies. A huge head goes under the water. A long time passes. Then the head rises and water streams off the antlers and gushes out of a half-open mouth filled with greens. The head shakes, sending arcs of spray across the pond. Silver droplets tinkle onto the water's surface as a long jaw chews, moving sideways. The humming of flies returns.

A moose will dive down 18 feet for a good bite of pond weed and float up tail-first while it's munching. Valves in its nostrils keep the water out of its nose. A moose swims with its entire head above water. It can swim for miles, and almost as fast as two people can paddle a canoe.

A moose can move even faster in water that would sink you to your ears. That's only belly-high to a moose. With her long legs pumping like pistons under her large, dark body, a cow moose hurrying to protect her calf in shallow water looks like a living locomotive. Those stilt-like legs work the same way in three or four feet of mud or snow. Moose rarely panic, even if they get stuck. They just rest, bat their ears at the flies (or snowflakes), and then lumber on. Moose are like that.

A moose in a hurry usually trots. Moose can gallop up to 35 miles per hour, faster than cars go on city streets, but they rarely do. They don't often jump, either. With those long legs they can step over almost anything that's too wide to go around.

SMACK!
What was that?
A moose? No.
Look there on
the pond. It
was a beaver,
slapping its
tail. Like
moose, beavers
eat bark and
aspen and
maple twigs.
They cut down
and carry off
the same trees
that moose munch on. But beavers help moose, too. They make ponds
where moose can eat and cool off. And after the beavers leave, their ponds
drain away to become dry meadows where young aspens and birches and
maples grow. It's a pretty good deal for a moose.

An adult moose packs up to 50 pounds of leaves, twigs, stems, and bark each day into the four stomachs it carries around inside its big belly. Like cattle,

goats, deer, and other animals, called ruminants, moose depend on this four-part system to help them digest their vegetables.

In summer, moose continue to eat leaves and twigs as well as pond weeds. Sometimes they just want leaves. A moose will bite across a willow branch and slide his head toward the tip of the branch, stripping off the leaves in his mouth. After some chewing, but not much, he'll swallow this mouthful into his first stomach and strip off more leaves. Later he'll burp the leaves up for more chewing and swallow them to the second stomach, where he begins digesting them.

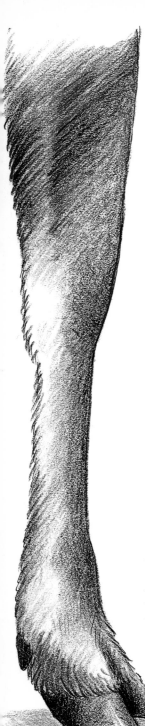

A moose may allow a girl or boy of average curiosity and adventurous spirit to walk up fairly close in the summertime. Sometimes too close. Don't get any ideas about rubbing that velvety soft muzzle. It isn't easy to alarm a moose, but if you get too close, the whole valley will hear about it. Moose are like that.

And don't think for a moment that the moose doesn't know you're nearby. Her eyes work independently, so she only needs one to keep an eye on you. See how her ears are pointed your way? She heard your lightest footsteps in the grass. And since most of the inside of her long face is nose, she noticed your scent a long time ago. You may not smell like a hungry bear, but you probably don't smell any better than one. To a moose, that is.

A bull moose grows his antlers all summer. A very young bull grows only spikes, but a big bull's rack of antlers may reach more than six feet across and weigh over 75 pounds. Growing antlers are covered by a soft, fuzzy skin called velvet. The velvet carries blood to the antlers, and the blood deposits calcium that makes bone. That's what an antler is—bone.

By September the antlers have finished growing, and the velvet dries and itches. Bulls rub it off against trees and thrash their racks in the bushes. You can see where a moose rubbed his rack. Other moose see this, too, and know there's a bull in the neighborhood.

Polished antlers shine like mirrors when they get wet. Watch the distant shore on sunny days for bright flashes. It could be a bull moose, or it could be the glint of sun off the canoe paddle of someone who has a good moose story to tell.

When my friend Phil came up to the north country one autumn, he wanted to see a moose. I told him I could find him one. So I took him over to our cabin on the river. We hiked up the ridge and saw tooth marks on the maples. We sneaked into the swamp and saw moose droppings. We crossed the clearing and found tracks and aspen sprouts with their tops browsed off. But we didn't find a moose. Phil said I wasn't much of a moose guide. I told him moose can be hard to find. "Moose are like that," I said.

Before supper I paddled the canoe up the river to catch some trout. After the sun went down and the air turned cold, a thick mist rose over the water. I heard a strange noise as I floated back down the river. It came out of the dark fog near our cabin. It sounded like a cross between a rusty car door hinge and a fog horn—deep, but with a squeak in it. Something like *HRRONK!* or *REEUMK!* I just knew it was Phil, hiding in the bushes and trying to grunt like a moose. (Phil is like that.) I made plans to sneak up and scare him.

But when I rounded the bend, I found a big bull moose instead of Phil. The moose stood in four feet of water, but I still had to look up at him from the canoe. He took a step or two, splashed his broad antlers in the river (first one side, then the other), then raised his dripping muzzle and bellowed. *HRRONK!* It was the beginning of the rut, or breeding season, and he was calling to other moose. I floated quietly past him and found Phil back at the cabin.

"Were you making that noise?" he asked me.

"Phil," I told him, "you missed your moose."

During the rut, prime bulls with big racks and years of experience pick fights with each other. You don't want a moose to get the wrong idea about you at this time of year. Bad-tempered bulls have chased many a trespasser up a tree. Watch from a distance. And if you ever meet a big bull face to face in the fall, remember this piece of advice: Don't mess with a moose.

A rutting bull stares at his challenger and circles him with stiff, confident steps. (Young bulls get nowhere when they try this. They just have to wait and grow.) Tension builds, moose heads lower, and antlers bang together like trees falling into each other. Usually one bull wins the fight before hurting the other one badly.

The cow stands quietly nearby in a place she has selected. She awaits the attention of the winner. The bull was fighting so he could be with her. After the rut, in November and December, the big bulls drop their antlers. Smaller bulls who didn't use theirs as much carry them as late as March. Dropped antlers disappear quickly, gnawed by mice and squirrels that recycle the calcium into their own bones.

Now it's winter. There's a moaning in the air. Wolves howling? No, not this time. Just the arctic wind. At 40 below zero, frost stings right through your warmest moosehide mittens and your heaviest boots. Your breath would freeze right to your beard, if you had one. Ice covers the ponds, and snow buries the bushes. Lush summer foods are gone now. Moose have moved to drier forests, where they browse on tough, leafless winter twigs that are less nourishing and harder to digest.

When the snow reaches belly-high, moose take shelter in stands of fir and hemlock. They may gather in groups now and stay sheltered in this winter cover for days. They browse on fir boughs or nearby willows and nap in the snow in their thick winter coats. Where food is scarce and winters are hard, moose eat all the fir boughs they can reach. In this winter range you'll see a browse line where no green twig is left below ten feet off the ground.

Most moose survive the long north-country winters, but they pay a price. By the time spring melts the frost and brings new plant growth (moose food!), a moose has lost one-third of its body weight. Imagine losing one-third of your weight. You'd look skinnier. So does a moose in May.

Last year's calf, a year old, gets the surprise of its life this spring. Its mother suddenly nips and kicks at it, sending it away. She prefers to give birth again in private. The yearling may rejoin its mother later in the year, or it might wander off. Yearlings are the most adventuresome moose when it comes to discovering new places to live.

In spring and summer, many people watch for moose near highways. Moose like to lick the salt that is spread on roads through the winter. Some moose, especially those adventuresome yearlings, wander across roads where drivers don't expect them. A driver can't always see a dark moose at night. This isn't good for the moose. It isn't good for drivers, either.

About one million moose live in North America today. One hundred years ago, fewer moose lived on this continent, mostly because people had killed too many. Today hunters continue to hunt moose (but not too many). Bears and wolves eat moose calves. Yet moose are returning to their former homes along the southern border of their range, where more people live. Here, believe it or not, deer carry the greatest threat to moose.

Deer live across the continent and north to the southern edge of moose range. A little parasite called the brain worm infects both deer and moose. When a deer has this disease, it stays healthy. You'd never even know it had brain worm. But when the brain worm infects a moose, it causes damage. The infected moose loses control, walks blindly into things, becomes paralyzed, and finally dies. A moose living around deer can be infected by the parasite at any time. The brain worm—and the heat, too—keep moose from expanding their range southward out of the northwoods.

Where I live, in New Hampshire, moose are coming back after being gone for many years. If you lived here, you might get a visit from one of those adventurous yearlings one May morning. Imagine a wild moose looking into the window of your cabin. But don't expect it to stay very long. What if it saw another moose's head sticking out of the wall over the fireplace? Or, even scarier yet, what if it saw a gangly little creature in a wool shirt and boots, looking back through the window with a mouthful of corn flakes?

What would a moose do then? Well, probably just trot over to the edge of the woods and look back at you with at least one eye. Maybe with both. Then it would march right down to the bug-filled marsh for a bite of aspen, as though nothing unusual had happened. As though it never even saw you.

Moose are like that.

GLOSSARY

Antler: A bony growth on the head of animals like moose and deer; antlers grow in pairs and are often branched (page 8).

Browse: To graze or feed on the tender shoots, twigs, and leaves of trees and shrubs (page 12).

Defensive: Serving to protect and defend against attack (page 19).

Dewlap: A loose fold of skin hanging under the necks of certain animals, such as moose (page 8).

Grazing: Feeding on grass and other vegetation (page 12).

Guard hairs: Long, coarse hairs that form a protective covering over the underfur of an animal (page 20).

Muskeg: A North American bog with sphagnum moss (page 5).

Muzzle (n): The part of an animal's head that projects forward and contains the nose and jaw (page 12).

Parasite: An animal or plant that lives in or on a different animal or plant, getting benefits from the host (page 44).

Prime bull: A mature male moose between the approximate ages of six and twelve (page 38).

Repellant: Something that drives something else away (page 21).

Ruminants: Hoofed animals with 3- or 4-chambered stomachs; ruminants chew their cud as part of the digestive process (page 29).

Spikes (n): The unbranched antlers of young moose or deer (page 32).

Velvet: The soft skin that covers and nourishes developing antlers (page 32).

Yearling: An animal one year old or in its second year of life (page 42).

ADULT-CHILD INTERACTION QUESTIONS

These are questions designed to encourage young readers to participate in further study and discussion of moose.

1. Do both male and female moose have antlers?

2. How is a moose like a caribou, another member of the deer family that also lives in the northern part of North America? How is it different?

3. How can a moose find and identify food under the water?

4. The moose was considered a good omen, or sign of things to come, by American Indians called Algonquians. Can you think of other animals that are considered good or bad omens?

5. How many states in the United States have a population of moose? Which states are they?

6. How can a moose use its antlers to help it survive during winter?

MORE BOOKS TO READ

Blue Moose and Return of the Moose by Daniel Pinkwater (Random House)
Meet the Moose by Leonard Rue and William Owen (Dodd)
The Moose by Mark Ahlstrom (Crestwood House)
Moose by Jenny Markert (Child's World)
Moose by Judy Ross (Grolier)
Moose by Jack D. Scott (Putnam Publishing Group)
Moose on the Loose by Ann and John Hassett (Down East)

VIDEOS

Animals of North America (Centron)
Mammals (Coronet)